mentees. The strategic approach outlined in this handbook will empower mentors to unlock their full potential and guide their mentee to their professional aspirations."

Larry Chloupek, *Co-Founder of Chloupek Consulting Services and Contractor for National Institute of Mental Health*

I0111430

ASPIRE TO
INSPIRE

ABC HANDBOOK

FOR THE ULTIMATE
MENTOR EXPERIENCE

DocUmeant *Publishing*
244 5th Avenue
Suite G-200
NY, NY 10001
646-233-4366
www.DocUmeantPublishing.com

Published by
DocUmeant Publishing
244 5th Avenue, Suite G-200
NY, NY 10001
646–233–4366

Edited by Sara Llansa Petty

Cover Design, Illustrations, and layout by DocUmeant Designs
www.DocUmeantDesigns.com

Library of Congress Control Number: 2024943108
ISBN: 9781957832425

What People Are Saying

"Michelle Jack knows the difference between having good intentions and setting achievable goals. Her book, *Aspire to Inspire* brings that wisdom to the mentoring relationship, where many people want to do well but may not know how to make the most of their mentoring experience. Each chapter tackles a different stage of the mentoring process and allows people to think critically and systematically about their own strengths, weaknesses, and experiences, offering an invaluable guide to effective mentoring."

Mary R. Rose, *Director of Human Dimensions of Organizations and Professor of Sociology at the University of Texas at Austin*

"Mentoring has often been viewed as an art which is difficult to describe and define, and even harder to assess in terms of effectiveness. Yet, most would intuit that mentoring is something that could and should create more accomplished leaders. Many successful leaders want to give back and help to create the next generation of great leaders by offering to mentor, but where to begin? Michelle's *Aspire to Inspire* handbook (which complements her *Inspire to Aspire* playbook) provides a logical framework to help mentors efficiently and effectively do their part towards successful mentoring engagements, including possessing a toolkit to understand their own keys to success. Ultimately, the fruitfulness of mentoring needs to be owned by the mentees but Michelle's handbook provides mentors with a partnership approach to chart a collaborative mentoring pathway with mentees. As someone who has been a mentor for many years, I wish I had had Michelle's *Aspire to Inspire* handbook when I began mentoring!"

David Swift, *Chairperson of the Board of OmniMax International and P1 Service Group, Advisory Board Member of The Edgewater Funds and President and CEO of Swift Consulting Services. Former Chairman or Chief Executive Officer of multiple public and private organizations.*

"I am thoroughly impressed with the mentoring handbook my colleague, Michelle Estades Jack, authored. This comprehensive guide is engaging, practical, and instrumental in helping mentors add significant value to their mentees' journeys. It offers actionable insights and strategies that unlock commitment, ensuring that mentors and mentees maximize the productivity of their investment. Whether you are a seasoned mentor or just beginning, this handbook provides the tools and guidance to foster meaningful and impactful mentoring relationships. I highly recommend it to anyone serious about making a positive difference through mentoring."

Cyndee Lake, *Chief Purpose Officer and Co-Founder of Blank Page*

"Mentoring can be one of the most fulfilling experiences in your professional career. *Aspire to Inspire: The ABC Handbook for the Ultimate Mentor Experience* transforms the traditional vague advice approach into a structured and collaborative process that maximizes a mentee's results and the mentor's confidence. From aligning mentoring goals, preparing for the initial meeting, and even the tricky step of formally ending a mentorship, this book will serve as your guide for every step along the way."

John Green, *Senior Vice President, Daikin Comfort Technologies North America*

"I read Michelle Jack's *Aspire to Inspire* over the weekend. *Aspire to Inspire* is a transformative guide to mentorship, weaving together powerful stories and practical advice to elevate both mentors and mentees. This book is a must-read for anyone looking to unlock their full potential and inspire others to do the same. A brilliant resource that will leave you motivated and empowered."

Rob Andrews, *Chairman and Chief Executive Officer of Allen Austin Consultants In Retained Search & Leadership Advisory*

"Our perspective in life is greatly influenced by our circumstances and the people who pour into us. Reflecting on those who invested their time and wisdom in me, I saw a pattern of genuine interest, consistency, and a willingness to speak the truth even when it was painful to hear. My mentors made it look effortless and made me feel valued and important in the process.

"Decades later, it is now my turn to give to the next generation of young women. As motivated, hungry to learn, and ready to take on the world, young females come into my orbit, I realize that the task and privilege of mentoring are easy at first, but grow more challenging as the days, weeks, and years progress. I also realize that the conversations hold just as big a mirror into my life as they do a window into theirs. That is not easy to face sometimes. And, when things get "not easy," one generally tries to retreat. But with tools such as a playbook, *Inspire to Aspire* and handbook, *Aspire to Inspire* keeps me in the game and at the table when things get hard and recommendations on how to take relationships deeper and how to encourage and inquire amid growing experiences are invaluable.

"I have learned how to use these tools to not only engage young mentees but to also keep myself engaged which helps me mentor more effectively and remain consistent. It also helps me gauge when I have reached my limit with my mentee and need to enlist others to carry on the progress . . . which can be personally humbling but, if honest, will yield the best outcome for everyone involved."

Becca Schwinger, *Director of Parents and Community, University of Austin, Member of Human Dimensions of Organizations Board, Christ the King Presbyterian Church Community Leader and Volunteer.*

"As a former mentor, I can wholeheartedly endorse the *Aspire to Inspire, the ABC Handbook for Ultimate Mentor Experience*. This invaluable resource provides a clear and engaging roadmap that transforms the mentorship journey. The handbook offers practical, hands-on guidance that will significantly enhance the mentor's ability to cultivate and inspire

To a great mentor and servant leader who taught me to "trust but verify," set REAL short-term and long-term goals, and know when to, and not to, put the headband on (Rambo reference).

Contents

PART 3

CORE CONNECTIONS: GLOBAL VIEW   83

ADDITIONAL RESOURCES   101

Acknowledgment

I WOULD LIKE to express my deepest gratitude to all the incredible individuals who generously shared their stories and insights for this book. Your experiences and thoughtfulness provide invaluable lessons that will undoubtedly inspire and guide future mentors.

To each of you who contributed, Lister Carbon, Nick Belcher, Larry Chloupek, Lauro Campos, Rob Andrews, and others, thank you for your commitment to our future leaders. Your dedication to nurturing the next generation of leaders is a testament to the profound impact that mentorship can have. Your stories of triumphs and challenges, along with your candid reflections, have enriched this book immeasurably.

It is my sincere hope that this compilation of your wisdom will serve as a beacon for those embarking on their mentoring journeys. Together, we are creating a legacy of mentorship that will resonate for years to come.

Thank you for your trust, honesty, and willingness to share. Your contributions are the heart and soul of this book.

Sincerest gratitude to Sara Llansa Petty who not only edited this work but also challenged the flow and clarity of it. Special thank you to Jenn Chloupek, the coauthor, who guided and mentored me through this process.

With heartfelt appreciation,

Michelle Jack

Introduction

ULTIMATE MENTORSHIP IS a transformative journey not only for the mentee but also for the mentor. The mentor's aspiration to inspire others is their legacy woven into the fabric of an ultimate mentee experience. A mentor, who embodies and lives their values, serves as a beacon, guiding their mentee through the intricate paths of professional growth. The mentor becomes a living example of authenticity, setting a standard for navigation and wisdom that leaves an indelible mark on the mentee's journey.

The mentor possesses rich experiences and, through creative problem solving, inspires and challenges the mentee to explore uncharted territories of possibilities. This collaboration extends beyond conventional boundaries, cultivating a mindset of previously unimaginable aspirations and broader perspectives. When successful, the mentorship experience becomes a catalyst for self-advocacy and self-determination that enriches and fortifies the mentee's future successes.

A mentor's impact is further magnified when they embody authentic leadership. Thoughtful consideration revolves around the question: Is my mentor inspiring me towards my aspirations of leadership excellence? Ultimate mentors do not just teach skills but also inspire mentees to cultivate their unique leadership styles, fostering the emergence of future leaders and mentors.

The mentor's legacy is defined not just by the mentor's personal accomplishments but also by their impact on their mentee's aspirations and future achievements.

How it Works

Mentorship partnerships vary from awkward experiences or complete failures to rewarding and successful. Why do mentorships fail? What are some of the common components of these awkward partnerships?

Mentors feel the pressure to do most of the work, such as dragging out of the mentee what they are looking for, finding books, topics, or exercises for the mentee to perform. Some mentors even feel that they are expected to entertain the mentee or act as a counselor. Something that could have such value becomes cumbersome and time consuming for the mentor.

Mentees are driven to seek mentorship to continue their development and professional growth. However, there is rarely a defined process for mentorship, and mentees are hindered by not knowing what they want in a mentorship experience. They need a plan that is clear and actionable to achieve their aspirational success.

A rewarding mentorship experience is one that is easy to execute with clear expectations. What if there were an easy to execute and clear process for both the mentor and mentee that resulted in the ultimate mentorship experience?

Welcome to the *Aspire to Inspire Handbook,* referred to as "Handbook" for the rest of this publication. This Handbook is designed for the mentor to facilitate the ultimate mentorship experience and is meant to complement the *Inspire to Aspire Playbook,* **specifically designed for the mentee**. For the rest of this Handbook, we will refer to the *Inspire to Aspire Playbook* as "Playbook." These books complement each other with similar material; however, can be used separately, as well.

In this Handbook, you will find reflective activities, discoveries, and revelations to help you gain a deeper understanding of yourself as a mentor.

Included are:

> » Mirrored materials from the Playbook.
> » A proposed timeline to guide you and your mentee through the experience with a defined beginning and end.
> » A Mentorship Tracker, midterm, and final calibration tools designed to help manage the process.

This Handbook is designed to maximize both your and your mentee's time and energy.

Your inspiration to share your knowledge, experience, and insights, as well as your reflection upon why you want to inspire, coupled with a guide to structure your relationship with your mentee will make the mentorship experience easy and clear. So many times, mentors want to help, but the mentee may not know WHERE to start. Mentees are excited to have a mentor and learn from someone they aspire to be; however, the experience can be intimidating and/or frustrating. Perhaps the mentee knows the WHAT, "to aspire in their career," but they do not know WHY or HOW.

Here's what our research found. Many programs do a great job of capturing the interest of mentors and mentees and may even provide matching services, but where they fall short is in not providing a process to guide the experience that inspires dialogue and actionable steps. The culmination of the Handbook and Playbook is a process that is simple and actionable for the ultimate mentorship experience.

Handbook Sections and How the Handbook Mirrors the Playbook

This Handbook, along with the Playbook, are tailored for the mentee and meant to be guided by the mentor. There are three sections in each book. The three main sections are: A) core Awareness, B) core Behaviors, and C) core Connections.

First, we start with core Awareness as you prepare for the partnership. In this section, we discover why you want to be a mentor, your values, what makes you a good mentor, and your vision as a mentor to prepare for the chemistry meeting, where you and the mentee begin working together. The first three sections of the Handbook and the first four sections of the Playbook are designed to be completed independently before you launch the partnership in the first meeting, the Chemistry Meeting.

Core Behaviors is where the mentee does the work and where you will see a mirror of the Playbook. The **I2A** designation are questions or direct representations of sections in Inspire **(I)** to **(2)** Aspire **(A)**. **I2A** indicates specific sections lifted from the Playbook and are provided as a reference in this Handbook.

In the core Behavior's section of the Playbook, the mentee completes a discovery assessment to determine which three to four core Behaviors to prioritize as topics of individual sessions with you. Each topic has activities and reflective spaces for the mentee to prepare for their session with you that includes embedded questions, or "Question for Mentor", for the mentee to ask you. These embedded questions are included in the Handbook.

After each activity from the Playbook, the Handbook includes a section for Mentor Reflection, so that you can reflect on the section and provide your views or thoughts prior to or during the session. A "Suggested Mentor Question" is provided as a prompt for you to use with your mentee that relates to that activity.

Before you launch into the final section, core Connections, a midterm calibration tool is provided to ensure you and your mentee's aspirations and expectations are aligned. Encourage your mentee to complete the assessment prior to your session. This will give you and your mentee space and time to check in on expectations and move forward.

The final section, core Connections, is when the mentee will reflect on four global topics and select one or two topics to focus on. You and your mentee will determine next steps, perform a final calibration, and initiate a partnership sunset. This section will be three to four sessions depending on the number of global topics chosen.

It is recommended that your mentorship sessions occur every two weeks to allow time for the activities and reflection in between sessions.

The resources section includes a proposed time-line, an example of the mentee's tracker page to summarize inspirations and note new material, and a timeout reveal to get to know each other on a personal level. Encourage your mentee to have this completed as part of their homework to maximize both your and your mentee's time and energy.

What is Your Role?

Let us take this opportunity to understand the difference between a mentor, a coach, and a sponsor. This will help you understand if a mentor is really what your mentee needs. Included are "Their Story" segments after each role for clarification.

A mentor is a trusted advisor who guides the mentee. Mentors serve as beacons, guiding the mentee through the intricate paths of personal and professional growth. Mentors offer advice based on experiences they have had in their careers as they are usually senior to the mentee. A mentor stands as a leader in their field and imparts not only practical knowledge but also instills the qualities of visionary and thought leadership. They become mentors who do not just teach skills but also inspire mentees to cultivate their unique leadership styles, fostering the emergence of future leaders. The mentorship becomes a transformative journey, leaving an enduring imprint on the mentee's life. The mentorship is based on trust, aligned values, commitment, and mutual respect.

Their Story

Alex has worked in the organization for a short time and is excited to show their value. Their aspirations transcend beyond their vision, and they are unsure how to get there. Their manager is great and relatively new to their role. Alex desires guidance from someone who is accomplished and manages a global team. Alex believes that mentorship would provide visibility with other senior leaders within the organization. Alex seeks a mentor who has influence in the organization and can share their experiences and advice.

Jordan is on the executive staff. Recently, Jordan's organization was acquired by a private equity firm. They aspire to become CEO of either this organization or another. Jordan has strong relationships with peers and the CEO; however, they are not sure where they fit in the new organization. Jordan also feels that their values may not be in alignment with the new management. Jordan feels alone and would benefit from a mentor to be a sounding board, provide advice, and challenge them.

A coach is engaged by you or your organization to focus on behaviors or skills that are hindering their client. Coaches focus on performance, personal and/or professional growth, and usually have specific areas of expertise. The coach provides tools based on the needs of the client to achieve the client's aspirations. The focus is usually targeted on areas of development, such as communication, decision making, prioritization, conflict management, and other non-technical skills. The relationship is usually for a specified period with a specified end goal that is funded by either their client or the client's organization.

Their Story

Taylor is the chief operation officer at an electronics manufacturing organization. Taylor has worked for the company for over 20 years and has risen through the ranks by being no nonsense and results oriented. Recently, their team has been stretched to include more organizational responsibilities. Taylor takes on much of the work and is short with the team, sometimes to the point of abuse. Taylor's team has vocalized this as a concern, and Taylor's manager, along with human resources, believes a coach could help them understand the impact of their behavior and provide Taylor with reflective tools and a space to evolve.

Daryl is a kindhearted and soft spoken manager. Daryl's team absolutely loves them; however, Daryl struggles to hold the team accountable and avoids conflict at all costs. Daryl's leader sees this as a developmental opportunity and recommends Daryl for a leadership program within the company that provides coaching tools for new leaders. Daryl will learn about accountability, setting clear expectations and how to resolve conflicts in a way that stays true to themselves.

A sponsor is a senior-level advocate who actively supports the individual's advancement. They use their influence to provide opportunities and visibility. The focus of the sponsor is to help the individual advance their career by recommending them for projects and opportunities that provide visibility and promotions. A sponsor could be a manager or a person with a higher-level position with influence. A sponsor could also express what is missing or deficient if that person has not achieved their aspirations and may make recommendations for further development, such as mentorship, coaching, leadership development or skills development. If a sponsor understands their team and other high potential team members, they can pitch those names during the closed-door meetings where succession planning, organizational changes, or high-visibility projects are discussed.

Their Story

Nissan is ambitious and is willing to take on any task to completion. Nissan works well with colleagues but is still relatively new to the organization. Nissan attends events and makes it a point to meet other leaders in the organization. Nissan is very interested in an opportunity and needs a sponsor who knows who they are, how they are suited for this role, and can speak to their attributes as opportunities arise.

~~~~~~

Casey has worked for the company for ten years and has progressed, in their opinion, slowly. Casey currently has a small team and aspires for their manager's position or a position of greater authority. Casey interviewed for the position when their manager was promoted but did not get the role. Now, Casey is considering their next step and would benefit from a sponsor to advocate for them.

Therapy

As more organizations focus on mental health in the workplace, it is important to understand the difference between mentorship and therapy. Therapy is a professional relationship between a licensed mental health professional i.e., therapist and client that focuses on emotional, psychological, or behavioral issues that cause distress or impair the client's life. Signs that a therapist may be more appropriate could be if the mentee shows signs of persistent emotional distress, difficulties coping with life changes, unhealthy coping mechanisms, trauma, chronic physical symptoms, or is consistently over-whelmed or stressed.

This program is based on experiences of the authors and is in no way to be considered therapy. A mentor, coach, or sponsor does provide guidance, support, or advice; however, they provide counseling that is or can be perceived as therapy.

Stories Told/Lessons Learned

EVERY TIME THEY walked into my office, I checked to see if they'd been crying. Seemed like no matter what we worked on; it was not enough. Sometimes, my suggestions, which I thought were simple and easily executable, became triggering and emotional. I doubted my ability as a mentor. I began to dread my mentorship sessions with my mentee. What was I thinking?

Lesson Learned

Sometimes, you are not qualified, and it is OK to say, "Let's take a break and come back at a later time," or "This is out of my area of expertise."

• •

Now that we have defined these roles, how will you use this information to guide your mentee? How will you distinguish the roles to ensure you are in the role you signed up for?

....

....

....

"IF YOUR ACTIONS
INSPIRE OTHERS TO
DREAM MORE, LEARN
MORE, DO MORE, AND
BECOME MORE, YOU
ARE A LEADER."

–JOHN QUINCY ADAMS

Part 1

Core Awareness: Prepare for the Partnership

Activity 1: Discovery
Activity 2: Core Values
Your Pivotal Story
Activity 3: The Mentor's Role
Activity 4: Calibration Meeting

CORE AWARENESS
Prepare for Partnership

Stories Told/Lessons Learned

PALMS SWEATING, BODY tense my ski instructor/mentor, Ryan, requests the lift operator to reduce the speed of the lift chairs to allow for those less experienced. Ryan had explained how to put both poles in your left hand as you look over your left shoulder to watch for the lift chair and to use your right for support. He said, "As you feel the chair, slowly sit, and you will be OK. I'll be right there beside you." OMG . . . 1st time on a lift, stomach churning and the biggest grin from ear to ear. I could not have done this without Ryan. Ryan, the ski mentor, who used their experience to help mentees achieve their aspirations through guided inspiration every day.

Trust was established as I listened closely to how to get off the lift. Ryan explained, "Keep your ski tips up. They will naturally align with the plateau of the launch pad. Once they are parallel, slowly stand with a bit of a forward lean. You got this!" I did it! (BTW . . . I did it again to prove it was not a fluke before enjoying some well-deserved hot cocoa with extra marshmallows!)

Lesson Learned
Trust is key to mentorship

• •

))) Activity 1: Discovery

What's In It for the Mentor

Ultimate mentorship becomes a transformative journey not only for the mentee but the mentor as well. The mentor's aspiration to inspire others is their expertise and legacy woven into the fabric of an ultimate mentee experience. A mentor who embodies and lives their truth serves as a beacon that uses a goal-oriented and futuristic approach to guide their mentee through the intricate paths of personal and professional growth. The mentor becomes a living example of authenticity and effective communication that is both empathetic and patient.

Your legacy and wisdom transcends beyond your success and onto the success of your mentee and future mentees. Just think back to your mentors, how did they shape the mentor you are today? Where would you be without their wisdom, constructive feedback, encouragement, network, and truths?

By using this process, your mentee will be prepared, and you will not have to do all the work.

Mentor Effectiveness Assessment: Nurturing Growth and Inspiring Excellence

Your commitment to the mentorship journey inspires others. This assessment is designed to help you reflect on essential qualities of an effective mentor and your inspiration as a mentor. Consider each quality carefully and provide a self-evaluation for each to gauge your potential impact on your mentee's development. Further, expand on your reflection in the reality reveal section. Is this a strength of yours or an area for self-development?

Experience and Expertise: A good mentor has a wealth of knowledge and experience in the field or area you are interested in.

Effective Communication: A mentor should be an excellent communicator, capable of explaining complex concepts, providing constructive feedback, and actively listening to your concerns.

Empathy and Patience: Mentors should be understanding and patient, recognizing your challenges and helping you navigate them *without judgment*.

Availability: A mentor should be accessible and willing to dedicate time to your growth. This is a time commitment for you both, and each of you will have to be available for this to work.

Encouragement and Support: A good mentor should motivate and inspire you. They should believe in your potential and encourage you to strive for your goals.

Goal-Oriented: A mentor should help you set clear goals and provide guidance on how to achieve them. Your mentor should challenge you if you are missing your goals to understand the deeper why.

Networking Skills: Mentors can help you connect with other professionals in your field, expanding your network and opportunities. Who do they know? How can this help you learn more about them and you?

Honesty and Constructive Feedback: A mentor should be candid in their feedback, pointing out observed areas of strengths and areas for improvement while offering suggestions for growth. Mentees *are not looking for a cheerleader or a critic*.

Using the chart, rate your mentorship qualities using a 1-5 rating, where 1 is not sure and 5 is most prepared. What reality is revealed as you assess yourself?

Quality	Rating	Reality Reveal
Experience and Expertise		
Effective Communication		
Empathy and Patience		
Availability		
Encouragement and Support		
Goal-Oriented		
Networking Skills		
Honesty and Constructive Feedback		

Mentor Inspiration Reflection

In this section, you will take your self-reflection one step further to envision your inspiration to your mentee. You will reflect on your own character, collaborative spirit, leadership, and futuristic transformative abilities as these will prepare you for this journey with your mentee.

Character Development

How consistent are you in demonstrating integrity and upholding strong values in both personal and professional spheres? Are there instances when you respectfully challenge the status quo when it is not in alignment with your or your organization's values? Do you know which battles to fight? How would you use honest and constructive feedback with your mentee?

How would you use these traits in your mentorship?

....

....

....

....

....

....

....

Creative Collaboration

How do you foster creative collaboration as you encourage innovative thinking and a broader perspective? Fostering collaboration where you seek to understand, develop relationships, and align for a common goal vs. individualized thinking is an important skill. How do you use your network to foster creative collaboration and collective problem-solving?

How would you use these traits in your mentorship?

....

....

....
....
....
....
....
....

Leadership Development

How prepared are you to inspire your mentee's leadership journey, where their vision, self- actualization, and self-advocacy align with the vision of the organization. How will you use empathy and patience in your discussions with your mentee?

How would you use these traits in your mentorship?

....
....
....
....
....
....
....

Actualization of Future Self

Using your experience and expertise, how will you inspire your mentee's transformation through candid conversations, thoughtful advice, and experience-driven alternate points of view? How can you help them see the possibilities and set achievable goals?

How would you use these traits in your mentorship?

....

....

....

....

Reality Reveal

Reflect on your overall self-assessment and identify areas where you could further enhance your effectiveness as a mentor.

What are actionable steps you can take to strengthen your mentorship impact in each of the aforementioned qualities?

....

....

....

....

....

....

....

Self-reflection is a tool for growth. Your commitment to continuous improvement will not only benefit your mentee but also contribute to the broader landscape of mentorship excellence. As you continue this journey, you are now more prepared to guide your mentee through the most impactful relationship of their career.

Thank you for your dedication to fostering growth and inspiring excellence.

Mentor's Reference to Mentee's Playbook

As you think of your impact on your mentee, below are topics that are reflected in the Playbook and will be prioritized by your mentee. When you think of your experiences and appetite to inspire your mentee, which of the subsequent **12A** Discovery topics reflect your strengths and the areas where you have tangible experience and advice for the mentee?

....

....

....

....

....

12A Discovery – Mentee's Personal View to Prioritize

1. **Work and Home Friction**: Prioritization between work and home with competing demands on your time, energy, and space.

2. **Emotional Intelligence**: Awareness and ability to recognize and regulate emotions, especially in moments of high intensity.

3. **Getting Out of Your Own Head**: Sometimes we just cannot get where we want to go due to overthinking, fear, and/or self-doubt.

4. **Goal Setting**: Setting clear, achievable goals, creating action plans, and achieving those goals.

5. **Career Transitions**: Guidance on a potential role, a new role, or a role transition.

6. **Visibility and Influence**: Visibility and influence is paramount to aspirations of career development.

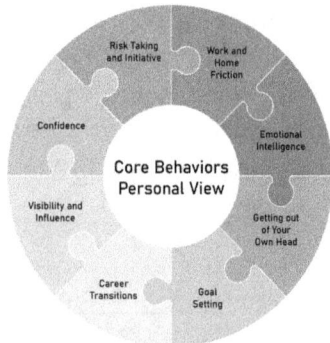

Risk Taking and Initiative / Work and Home Friction / Confidence / Emotional Intelligence / Core Behaviors Personal View / Visibility and Influence / Getting out of Your Own Head / Career Transitions / Goal Setting

7. **Confidence**: Self-confidence in a professional environment.

8. **Risk Taking and Initiative**: Ability to take risks and initiatives to expand outside of your comfort zone.

I2A Discovery – Mentee's Global View to Prioritize

1. **Networking:** Methods to expand your professional network and build meaningful relationships in your industry.

2. **Organizational Culture:** Identify, understand, and navigate organizational culture.

3. **Navigating Corporate Politics:** Understand how things get done, who to interface with on important topics, and how to navigate difficulties.

4. **Allyships:** Allies play a pivotal role in shaping organizational culture, driving innovation, and fostering a workplace where every individual feels valued and empowered to contribute their best

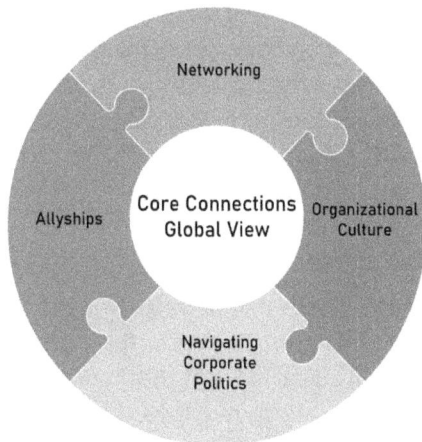

))) Activity 2: Core Values
(Same as I2A)

Your core values are your standards that are unique and intrinsic to you. They guide how you view the world and what inspires you. By identifying your core values, you gain insight into why things, situations, and relationships are more or less important, more or less exciting, or more or less frightening to you. They also provide an understanding of our uniqueness (not everyone has the same values or even the same definitions), which can lead to unintended conflicts and misunderstandings.

This activity will help you identify your core values. You will review your core values and consider how these values influence what is important to you. As you go through these values, there may be some that you aspire to; however, it is imperative that you identify your true values. At the end, you will assess how they show up in your life and work. You may even want to look up the definition of the value to see if that definition aligns with your value as defined and experienced by you.

Also, when you compare values with other individuals, you may notice that their definition of that value may be different than your own. When you meet with your mentee, compare values, and learn how your values and theirs align or differ. How are these values revealed in your and your mentee's personal and professional lives?

Below you will find a list of values. Be honest with yourself and rate each value based on the authentic you vs. the aspirational you. If your value is missing, there is space provided at the bottom of the table.

If you rate them all high or low, review them again and narrow your selection to four.

Rate Each Value on a Scale from 1 to 5.

1 – not important; 5 – must have

Value	Rating	Value	Rating
Achievement		Balance	
Adventure		Happiness	
Creativity		Health	
Courage		Peace	
Curiosity		Learning	
Growth		Self-discipline	
Authenticity		Community	
Compassion		Education	
Friendship		Freedom	
Love		Family	
Loyalty		Justice	
Respect		Service	
Trust		Teamwork	
Integrity		Spirituality	

Value	Rating	Value	Rating
Open-mindedness		Wealth	
Economic Stability		Security	

List Your Top Four Values

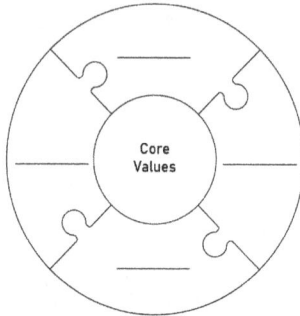

Your Pivotal Story

We all have a story and pivotal moments in our development both professional and personal that shape who we are today. As you think about your career and personal milestones, what were the pivotal moments? Pivotal moments could be education, roles, mentors, or personal changes, such as localities, relationships, or family development.

On the following page draw your pivotal story from the beginning of your professional journey to today. Identify moments or events that led you here.

As you reflect on your journey, your legacy transcends into your mentorship. How will you weave your story to inspire your mentee to achieve their aspirations?

What inspired you to become a mentor?

....

....

....

....

....

....

....

What attributes would your ultimate mentee exhibit?

....

....

....

....

....

....

....

Who were your mentors past or present? How did they inspire you?

....

....

....

....

....

....

....

....

What gives you the greatest energy and excitement as you think about mentorship?

....

....

....

....

....

....

....

....

....

....

How much time/energy can you commit to this mentorship?

What can you learn from your mentee?

⫸ Activity 3: The Mentor's Role

To Challenge and Encourage Self Advocacy

Your role in this partnership is to challenge, in a constructive way, and inspire the mentee to think about things differently. When you use questions that reveal a reality otherwise unseen, inspiration occurs, and aspirations are enabled.

In the "Art of Asking Smarter Questions" by Arnaud Chevallier, Frédéric Dalsace, and Jean-Louis Barsoux, they suggest that there are 5 types of questions: *investigative "how", speculative "what if", productive "now what", interpretive "so, what?",* and *subjective "what's unsaid?" Or "How can I help?"*

Throughout the activities in **I2A**, the mentee is asked to think about what is possible, what is known, and what ifs. Encourage this self-discovery, so that you can use your experience to broaden their perspective.

When you ask questions that are imaginative and simple, you provide space for your mentee to dig a little deeper. These inquisitive questions encourage self-reflection, promote learning and development, and encourage problem assessment and self-advocacy. These questions can also build trust and rapport with your mentee and model the use of questions as they seek to understand.

Below are sample questions for you to consider.

1. What is your biggest challenge right now?
2. What resources do you need to achieve your goals?
3. How can I support you in achieving your goals?
4. How have you overcome this in the past?
5. What steps have you taken thus far?
6. Where do you want this to go?
7. What is the best possible outcome?
8. What obstacles do you face, and how can you overcome them?
9. How can you approach the situation differently to achieve your aspirations?
10. What is the next step to move this forward?
11. What have you learned from this experience and how can you apply it in the future?
12. What are the potential risks involved in this decision, and what is your mitigation plan?

There are also a few simple prompts that lend space for the person to elaborate.

Those prompts are: And? Because? Tell me more.

You can even begin questions with an intro of "I am curious . . ." When you lead with "I am curious" it provides an introduction and is a substitute for "why" questions. "Why" questions may put your mentee in a defensive position and should be avoided if possible.

An example of this could be: "You mentioned a challenge with a person" "I am curious. Where do you think this comes from?" If they provide a simple response that does not provide insight, then ask, "And?"

Which questions would you use?

....

....

....

....

....

....

....

....

Leverage Your Experience and Expertise

How would you utilize your experience and expertise as you embark on this journey with your mentee?

))) Activity 4: Chemistry Meeting

Morgan's Story

The first year I worked with Morgan was difficult for both of us. My intention was to lead, and Morgan's was to keep their head above water by staying current with all tasks and requirements. Morgan was cautious of new reporting relationships and the thought of adding more tasks or a promotion was an undesirable proposition for them. Once Morgan understood that my motivation was to offer trust and prepare them to take over for me in the succession planning process, things became more comfortable. As we grew together over the first year, we both could see that our skills were not the same but highly complementary and functionally supportive.

When I thought about the areas that I could help Morgan grow in, what came to mind was:

1. Commit to daily planning and decide which tasks needed to be prioritized that day as opposed to set aside for another day;

2. Focus on these critical few tasks while working in a value stream to achieve completion and deadline success;

3. Always remain calm and take time to celebrate the daily gains and wins.

Morgan's efforts along with the skills that they already possessed translated into a promotion once

I departed the function. Morgan led their team-mates for many years and into retirement.

Lesson Learned

Meet mentee where they are at and offer hands-on support.

• •

First Meeting with Mentee

So, you are ready for the all-important chemistry meeting with your mentee. In this section, you will get to know each other, agree upon rules of engagement, and set mutual expectations for the ultimate mentorship experience. This first meeting is crucial and consists of three sections: get to know each other, rules of engagement, and expectations.

Get to Know Each Other

A chemistry meeting and rules of engagement, at the onset of this mentorship, might have benefited Morgan and their mentor. Each of you has performed self-reflective work up to this point. Now, it is time to share and see if you WANT to work together. This is a pivotal moment as trust starts here. Each of you will need to decide if there is an appetite for a mentorship relationship.

Take them through your pivotal moments that define where you are today and how you got there.

Perhaps explain how others have inspired you and why you are interested in mentoring them.

Alignment of Sections

- » **I2A** *Discovery:* What areas in the discovery section did your mentee prioritize? Does this align with your expertise and passion?
- » *Values:* Share a bit about your values and why they are important. Do you and your mentee have similar values? Do you define those values similarly?
- » **I2A** *Personal Vision:* They created a personal vision statement in **I2A**. Have your mentee share this with you.
- » **I2A** *Discovery Recap:* Is there anything that the mentee learned that they would like to share?
- » **I2A** *Ultimate Mentor:* What does the ultimate mentor look like for the mentee?

Rules of Engagement

This very important step is sometimes missed. Below, you will find suggestions for rules of engagement with alignment questions to ensure mutual understanding. Agree on the definition of words, such as confidentiality, honesty, and off limits. This creates alignment and trust in the relationship. Space is provided for you and your mentee to write in other rules of engagement that are not listed.

Frequency of Meetings and Commitment: How often should we meet? *We recommend every two weeks.* What happens if something interferes? What is our agreement to notify each other? How can we keep our commitments?

....

....

....

....

....

....

Time Commitment: Define your time commitment. What will our agreement be during and after this partnership? How long should this take? See Proposed Timeline in the reference section page 101. Example of Tracker is on page 104.

....

....

....

....

Communication Avenues: What is the best method to communicate? Chat, email, phone? Under what circumstance(s)?

Homework: The mentee is expected to do work between meetings. Assignments are laid out in the Playbook. What is the commitment regarding homework? What happens if homework is not complete? What if there are questions between sessions? How will the Mentorship Tracker be utilized?

Confidentiality: Define confidentiality. What is our confidentiality agreement during and after this partnership?

....

....

....

....

....

....

....

....

Honesty: Define honesty. What does honesty mean in this relationship?

....

....

....

....

....

....

....

....

....

Off Limits: What topics are off limits? How do we communicate off limit topics? These could also be defined as emotional triggers. Examples of these could be politics, personal information, religion, social media, etc.

....

....

....

....

....

(blank for you to add another rule of engagement)

....

....

....

....

....

....

....

....

....

(blank for you to add another rule of engagement)

....

....

....

....

....

....

....

Closure of Mentorship: What will our relationship look like after our mentorship has come to an end? Examples could be email, check-ins, coffee once per month/quarter, a phone call the 15th of each month, or "give me a call when you want to catch up."

....

....

....

....

....

....

....

....

Expectations

You and your mentee will likely have some ideas around expectations. This is an opportunity to calibrate these expectations to ensure alignment for the ultimate mentorship experience.

Create joint expectations regarding goals, time commitment, and success factors of mentorship.

What are our expectations of this mentorship?

At the end of this partnership, how would we measure success? *This may be a good opportunity to review the midterm and final calibration tools on page 76 and page 96.*

12A The following questions were provided to the mentee to ask the mentor.

» What specific goals or outcomes do you envision for our mentorship?
» How can you best support my professional growth and development?
» What key areas or skills do you hope to share or enhance through this relationship?
» Why are you interested in mentoring me? Share your vision and aspirations for this partnership.

I DO NOT KNOW ANYONE WHO HAS GOTTEN TO THE TOP WITHOUT HARD WORK. THAT IS THE RECIPE. IT WILL NOT ALWAYS GET YOU TO THE TOP, BUT IT SHOULD GET YOU PRETTY NEAR.

—MARGARET THATCHER, FORMER PRIME MINISTER.

Part 2

Core Behaviors: Personal View

(Mentee's Work, Mentors Advise and Guide)

Activity 1: Work and Home Friction

Activity 2: Emotional Intelligence

Activity 3: Getting Out of Your Own Head

Activity 4: Goal Setting

Activity 5: Career Transition

Activity 6: Visibility and Influence

Activity 7: Confidence

Activity 8: Risk and Initiative

Mid-term Calibration

Reflect and What's Next

CORE BEHAVIORS
Personal View from 12A

>>> **Activity 1: Work and Home Friction**

Avery's Story

I recognized very early on that we had to start from the beginning with Avery given that prior leaders had not properly invested in their development. What I realized, though, was that this individual had a desire to learn and contribute but was also hopeful for balance. What we often spoke about was the importance of communicating, putting in effort, and believing in the cause. Avery chose to welcome the challenge and put the work in. Our attempts at offering trust to one another became uneven at times simply due to the pressures and demands placed on them.

I felt certain that I could offer support to this individual within the topics of:

1. Technical know-how and methods understanding;
2. Working on necessary projects and reporting out on what mattered most and;
3. Helping them relearn how to remain calm and committed to managing priorities and therefore stress.

Their efforts were both sincere and actionable although we did debate quite frequently during our early days together. This leader performed extremely well by gaining added confidence, new functional skills, and internal customers. Avery continues to achieve to this day.

Lesson Learned

Create an environment that permits mistakes and remain patient as it is their journey.

• •

Avery wanted balance, but they were unsure how to achieve balance. We have been told about the need for a balance between work and home. *Spoiler alert: There is no such thing as balance. You are only one person. You are not a home person and a separate work person. Everything is competing for your time and energy, and supply is limited.*

What people experience is the friction between home and work. In both realms of life, some sacrifices are made as we prioritize conflicts and navigate the friction. With the added complexity of work from home and hybrid work, this can be even more of a challenge. Understanding your boundaries is the key to creating a balance between work and home.

12A

The mentee has been given questions about their workspace, rules, how they separate work and home, and even how they prioritize their health. They were given the tool "Stop, Start, Continue" to identify their plan. They were also encouraged to use "Did I do my best to . . . " to track their progress. See examples below:

Stop: To create appropriate boundaries and reduce friction between home and work, what will you stop doing? When will you stop?

Start: To create appropriate boundaries and reduce friction between home and work, what will you start doing? When will you start?

Continue: To maintain appropriate boundaries and maintain healthy friction between home and work, what will you continue?

They were also introduced to an accountability partner. An accountability partner is someone who holds them accountable. They were asked: "What part of the above "Stop, Start, Continue" will be most difficult to do? Who can help you and your plan succeed?"

To track progress, they were encouraged to use the below tool:

At the end of each day, rate yourself using a scale of 1 to 10. This tool is an inspiration from Marshall Goldsmith's tool in Triggers.

For Mentor Reflection

What are your views as it pertains to work and home friction? How are your views the same or different?

....

....

....

....

....

....

12A – Question for Mentor: *How do you manage home and work? What works well and what have you tried that just does not work?*

Potential Mentor Question: *How committed are you to this plan? How can I help you stay accountable? Who have you communicated this plan to, and how will they help you?*

≫ Activity 2: Emotional Intelligence

Joe's Story

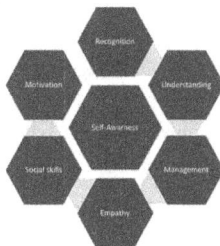

When I first met Joe, I realized that they had excellent skills, but their skills were overshadowed by a strong temperament. This caused Joe to have poor interactions with the team members, making it difficult to get things done. Joe was not aware that their behavior was the cause.

We focused on:

1. Joe needed to learn how to communicate with their team and colleagues. Joe needed to learn to modulate their voice and tone depending on the circumstances. Joe would use "gunshot" tonation when interacting with others. This did not help Joe build good relationships, create a collaborative environment, or get things done.

2. Joe needed to listen before they answered, expressed an opinion, or gave direction. This created a better environment for others as they felt "heard" instead of questioned or reprimanded. 2-way communication started to flow.

3. Joe needed to foster an environment of trust and recognize that, in many cases, the ideas of others are better than theirs.

After several months of working with Joe, they evolved into one of the best business unit managers of the organization, where results were sustained by true teamwork led by Joe. Joe was able to channel their energy in a more productive way and everything became easier.

Lessons Learned

Mentees may not be aware of how their actions hurt their success. Be honest with them even if they do not want to listen.

• •

Joe's story illustrates the importance of self-awareness. The term "Emotional Intelligence" first appeared in 1964. However, it gained popularity in the 1995 best-selling book *Emotional Intelligence* by Daniel Goleman.

If someone has high emotional intelligence, they possess skills that enable them to recognize, manage, and effectively use both their own emotions and those of others. Emotional intelligence is multifaceted and includes key components, such as emotion recognition, understanding, and management, as well as empathy, social skills, self-awareness, and motivation.

In this section, the mentee was asked to self-assess themselves using "No Issues", "Needs Improvement", or "Help me!"

12A Questions

Emotional recognition means that you can accurately identify your emotions and the emotions of others. You identify these emotions by using verbal and nonverbal cues. How do you know if you are upset or if others are upset?

Emotional understanding means that you understand the causes and consequences of various emotions in both yourself and others. How well do you react to your emotions or those of others?

Emotion management is the self-regulation of emotions. You can adapt to anger, stress, or other strong emotions without becoming overwhelmed and reactionary. How calm are you in stressful situations?

Empathy is the ability to sense and share the feelings of others. You have a genuine concern for the well-being of others, and are skilled in listening, offering support, and not judging. Can you meet the other person where they are instead of where you think they should be?

Social skills are the ability to communicate effectively, resolve conflict, and build positive relationships. You can navigate social situations with ease. How successful are you with conflict resolution and building positive relationships?

Self-awareness is just how it sounds. To be aware of how emotions affect you and how to deal with them. You have a clear and accurate perception of your strengths and weaknesses. Can you identify your strengths and weaknesses and how they affect those around you?

Motivation can be intrinsic or extrinsic. Intrinsic motivation is the ability to harness your emotions and focus on the task at hand even in the face of challenges. How easy is it for you to bounce back from setbacks or failures?

For Mentor Reflection

What are your views as it pertains to Emotional Intelligence? How are your views the same or different?

....

....

....

....

....

Potential Mentor Question: *When you think of these questions, which one stops you from achieving your aspirations?*

12A – Question for Mentor: *Where and when do you most struggle with these facets of emotional intelligence? What tools do you use, or how do you manage through these?*

>>> Activity 3: Getting Out of Your Own Head

Riley's Story

Riley was super smart, super motivated, and super doubted themselves.

When they did not get a promotion to lead a team, they assumed it was because of gender. It's difficult to combat the beliefs we hold so dear.

We worked through limiting beliefs and continued to work on "What are you afraid of?"

Riley was afraid of not having the answers to EVERYTHING!

They had to work through what was possible for them and realize that it is impossible to know everything. What was possible was to develop relationships with those that do, understand how each member of the team contributes, and that they do not have to do all the work.

I'm happy to report that not only did Riley get promoted, but they also have a strong team of their own and lead a cross-functional/global team very successfully.

Lesson Learned

No matter how much you believe in your mentee, they must believe in themselves for the mentorship to be effective.

Like Riley, so many of us are just stuck in our own heads. Even if you try to tell yourself "Mind over matter"; sometimes, that is not enough. The best way to get out of your own head is to figure out what is holding you back. Fear is the leading reason that individuals cannot get out of their own heads. Other reasons could be limiting beliefs or what could be perceived as imposter syndrome.

12A

The mentee has the following activities to prepare for this session.

What are you afraid of?

Fear comes in many forms: fear of looking stupid, fear of not having the answer, fear of the unknown, or fear that you are just not good enough.

So, when a person cannot get out of their own head, there is something that they are afraid of. They might be fearful of being in front of a room full of people, presenting information that they are not sure will be accepted, or leading a new team, project, or something they have never done before.

12A *Questions*

- » What are you afraid of?
- » How and when do these fears reveal themselves?
- » How do these fears stop you from fulfilling your aspirations?
- » What techniques have you tried to combat these fears that worked well or did not work?

Limiting beliefs:

Limiting beliefs are those beliefs that you are just not good enough. This may be from the words spoken to you, to others, or about others. This may be from behaviors you have witnessed

LIMITING BELIEFS   ASPIRATIONAL BELIEFS

1. ....
2. ....
3. ....
4. ....
5. ....
6. ....

1. ....
2. ....
3. ....
4. ....
5. ....
6. ....

or were subjected to, good or bad. Limiting beliefs may stem from internal comparison of yourself to others. These limiting beliefs can be debilitating. They can stop you from reaching your ultimate goals.

The mentee was asked to write limiting beliefs and rewrite them as aspirational beliefs.

12A Questions

What would your world look like if you replaced your limiting beliefs with your aspirational beliefs? What would have to happen?

Next time a limiting belief comes to mind, take note of where you are, what is happening, and who you are with. Then, practice with your aspirational belief. What challenges will you face with this aspirational belief? How can you conquer limiting beliefs?

Imposter syndrome:

Imposter syndrome refers to a psychological phenomenon in which individuals, despite external evidence of their competence, skills, or accomplishments, consistently doubt their own abilities and fear being exposed as frauds. People experiencing what can be perceived as imposter syndrome often believe that their success is a result of luck or other external factors, rather than their own

capabilities. They have an internalized fear of being "found out" as an imposter in their field or profession.

Imposter syndrome was first coined by psychologists Pauline R. Clance and Suzanne A. Imes.

12A Questions

» Do you often feel like your achievements are due to luck or external factors rather than your own abilities?

» Do you have difficulty internalizing your successes and feel that they are not a true reflection of your competence?

» Do you frequently worry that others will discover you are not as capable as they think you are?

» Do you set exceptionally high standards for yourself and fear you will fall short, even when you meet or exceed these standards?

» Do you downplay your accomplishments or attribute them to factors other than your own skills and hard work?

If you answered "yes" to any of these questions, describe the circumstance(s). Be specific about who, what, when, and where, as this may provide clues to which situations this is the most prominent for you.

For Mentor Reflection

What are your views as it pertains to getting out of your own head? How are your views the same or different?

....

....

....

....

....

....

....

Potential Mentor Question: *When you think of these areas, which one(s) stop(s) you from your aspirations? How?*

12A–Question for Mentor: *When have you experienced fear, limiting beliefs, or imposter syndrome? What did you do?*

))) Activity 4: Goal Setting

Skylar's Story

When I think about Skylar, what comes to mind was that they were a very caring manager and generous individual. We worked together for a turnaround manufacturer and learned early on that we both had similar beliefs. Skylar had many favorable attributes but, like most of us, needed to change some to bring added focus and discipline to their work style to become a more effective leader. Skylar's strong character and values allowed them to elevate their influence and gain employee commitment.

Areas that I felt I could help Skylar in included the following:

1. Emphasis on deadline importance;
2. Practice and demonstrate daily accountability;
3. Remain calm to maintain clear thinking.

They tended to build confidence in themself by muti-tasking assignments and projects, which resulted in missed deadlines and added stress. Given how busy this manager was when working on numerous needs and activities, they were not able to spend the appropriate coaching time with their direct reports and other subordinates. Task overload would cause Skylar to be late to meetings, which, in turn, added to both our frustrations. Once Skylar taught themself to focus on the critical few, be highly disciplined regarding executing to schedule and meeting their promises, we together grew in our trust and relationship, resulting in a better outcome.

Lesson Learned

Offer frequent coaching feedback and guidance to ensure alignment.

• •

Similar to Skylar, mentees may struggle to set and achieve goals. You may have a different goal-setting process. Review your process with your mentee.

12A Questions

Reflect on your ability to set and achieve your goals. Perhaps you are good at setting goals, but they are not achievable. Many times, our intent is not to fail to achieve our goals, but something may get in the way. As you set goals, are they fair and doable? What help or collaboration is needed for success? *Tip: Goals that align with your values and passions tend to be more successful.*

> » When did you set a goal and failed to meet it? Describe the goal.
> » Now, let us look at this goal with fresh eyes. Was it a S.M.A.R.T. (Specific, Measurable, Achievable, Relevant, Time-bound) goal? How was it defined by these criteria? How

would you revise the failed goal to be S.M.A.R.T.?

» Describe the benefits of setting a goal using the SMART format.

» How can you boost your motivation when you work towards a goal?

» What are the obstacles to setting and achieving your goals?

Create a S.M.A.R.T. goal for something that you want to accomplish in the short-term.

For Mentor Reflection

What are your views as it pertains to goal setting? How are your views the same or different?

....

....

....

....

....

....

Potential Mentor Question: *What part of this is difficult?*

12A – **Question for Mentor**: *What process do you use to create and maintain goals?*

))) Activity 5: Career Transition

Cameron's Story

I have mentored many individuals during my professional career. Several of my mentees have stood out. Cameron was one.

Cameron was younger than most of my mentees, but we connected on both a professional and personal level. Cameron was working while obtaining a college degree. They were in a very menial job, which was not utilizing their strengths. They were also not happy in their position.

We started at ground zero: getting to know each other and learning about their interests, strengths, and weaknesses. Our first goal was to get out of the dead-end position and find one that better suited their strengths and career interests. We accomplished this goal.

After a lot of thought and discussion, Cameron decided on a career track. We worked on a career development plan and what would make them a top candidate for positions in the years to come. We discussed various jobs to apply for, specialized experience, and education.

With Cameron's hard work, determination, and a mentor by their side, I am proud to say Cameron is in a senior position in their professional field and highly respected.

Lesson Learned

Stick to a plan even when there are days you may want to give up.

• •

Similar to Cameron, your mentee may be in a career transition. These transitions could be due to a promotion, industry shift, economic factors, changes in education, or geographic changes.

In the Playbook, these career transitions were categorized as considering, transitioning, or transitioned.

12A Questions

Considering

If you are considering a career transition, create your dream job description with as much detail as possible, including anticipated position requirements.

>   » Now, reflect on your proposed job description. What is missing? How does this compare with your current role?
>   » What roles within your organization align with this job description? What experience, skills, or knowledge deficiencies do you have, if any?
>   » What should your next steps be? How can you obtain an understanding of the expectations for the role?

» If there is not a role that aligns with your aspirations, where can you investigate? How can your mentor help you?

Transitioning

Transitioning from one role to another within the same or a new organization requires patience, humility, and a willingness to learn. You can start this process by meeting with your team, peers, customers (both internal and external), and your manager.

Using the three simple questions: what you know, what you do not know, and what you think you know about the role and expectations of the role, can prepare you to have one-on-ones with your new team.

Practice using the above three simple questions.

» What did using this reveal? Was it similar among your teammates?
» Which responses surprised you?
» How can you use this information to guide your communication with the team?

Other questions to ask stakeholders, such as internal customers, external customers, peers, and leadership could be:

» What is your expectation of this role?
» What are some complexities that I should understand that may not be apparent?

» What is your preferred form of communication?
» How can I best help you be successful?
» What priorities do you envision for the next 90 days?

Transitioned

You have already transitioned into a new role, and things could be better.

Have you shared your vision statement with stakeholders? Where do they fit into this vision statement? Use the three questions of what we should stop, start, and continue to create a dialogue with the team.

Write your vision and the challenges you see.

How would you communicate your vision and the challenges with your new team?

Use the "Stop, Start, Continue" technique to identify the issues that need attention. Then, using the "What is possible?" question, identify which steps are doable and possible to create a feedback loop with your team. Not everything will be possible, and that is OK. Concerns, as well as challenges, possibilities, or timelines around these concerns should be communicated. This creates a team that feels heard.

» What did the team think should be stopped? What is possible?

- » What did the team think should be started? What is possible?
- » What did the team think should be continued? What is possible?
- » What surprised you about these responses?
- » How can you use this information to guide your communication and changes within the team? How will you communicate in a way that shows your team that they were heard?

For Mentor Reflection

What are your views as it pertains to career transition? How are your views the same or different?

. . . .

. . . .

. . . .

. . . .

. . . .

. . . .

Potential Mentor Question: *Where are you in this process, and how can I help?*

12A – Question for Mentor: *Could you tell me about a great career transition and a not-so-great one you experienced? What would you have done differently?*

))) Activity 6: Visibility and Influence

Quinn's Story

Quinn approached me through LinkedIn. Initially surprised by the request to be mentored, as they were unknown to me, curiosity led me to understand what they hoped to gain from my specific experience.

During our discovery call, things became clear. Quinn was referred to me by a former mentee of mine. Quinn found me on LinkedIn and became intrigued by my Lean Six Sigma posts and career journey. Quinn saw this as the path to follow. I explained to Quinn that the path I traveled was my own, but I could certainly guide them. First, I needed to understand Quinn's priorities, values, and goals.

Quinn's response told me that they were ready. Quinn wanted to make a larger impact on the organization by building a Continuous Improvement culture and needed a mentor with this type of experience. We focused our bi-weekly calls on:

1. Education—Quinn would need Lean Six Sigma certifications to demonstrate credibility. I agreed to tutor them as well as show their company the potential ROI.

2. Demonstrating Value—Quinn needed to seek out initial improvement opportunities that were low-cost, easy to implement, and most impactful. I agreed to review their improvement ideas and help prioritize the projects most likely to get buy-in from Executive Sponsors.

3. Career Planning—Quinn knew that their influence over the organization's culture would be limited by their current role. We first identified the leadership level they aspired to reach and then outlined potential steps to get there.

By structuring the mentor/mentee relationship in this manner, Quinn and I were able to ensure each meeting added value.

Lesson Learned

Have a structured process to make it productive.

• •

Quinn wanted influence within their organization to achieve their aspirations. Your mentee may seek visibility and/or influence within their organization. Visibility is the level of recognition, awareness, and prominence an individual has within an organization. Visibility is an essential part of professional success, career advancement, and effective teamwork. Visibility can be achieved by delivering high-quality results, effectively communicating (both upwards and downwards), contributing to important projects, and networking. Visibility can be defined as creating a positive impact that benefits not only the individual but also the team and the organization.

I2A Questions

Visibility

> » How do you want the organization to see you?
> » Do you want the organization to see you as a team player, a go- getter, a knowledgeable leader, a high potential, someone who cares, a risk taker, or what?
> » What does that look like today?
> » Describe how you believe you are viewed today. Be specific as it could vary in different circumstances and even with different people.
> » What gaps appear in how you want the organization to see you and how you believe they see you today?
> » What steps can you take to close that gap? What is stopping you?
> » How can your mentor help you gain the visibility you are looking for?

Influence

Influence is the ability to affect the thoughts, decisions, actions, and opinions of others. Influence can drive positive change, garner support, and shape the direction of the company. Your ability to influence is based on your credibility, ability to communicate persuasively, relationship building skills, problem-solving, and teamwork. *Tip: Curiously observe others and how they influence.*

I2A Questions

- » How do you want to inspire others in the organization?
- » Are you at the influence level that you aspire to be? What would that look like? Describe an influential person who inspires you.
- » How would you assess this person on their credibility, ability to communicate persuasively, relationship building skills, problem-solving, and teamwork?

Rate yourself on the influence aspects below. This would be a great opportunity to request feedback from someone else. Compare your self-ratings to their ratings.

Aspect	Your Assessment	External Assessment	Gap
Credibility			
Persuasiveness			
Relationships			
Problem-Solving			
Teamwork			

I2A Questions

- » What insights did you gain from this experience?
- » Which have the largest gaps? What do you think is missing?
- » What steps can you take to close these gaps?

»   How would you use your influence to help yourself, others, and the organization?

For Mentor Reflection

What are your views as it pertains to visibility and influence. How are your views the same or different?

_____

_____

_____

_____

_____

_____

_____

_____

_____

_____

Potential Mentor Question: *What do you think is the number one reason for the gaps?*

12A – Question for Mentor: *How would you rate me on these aspects? What do you think is the one thing I could do to improve my visibility and influence?*

⫸ Activity 7: Confidence

Sam's Story

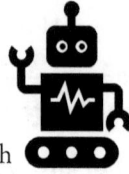

Sam was a phenomenal leader, though they didn't quite realize it at the time.

Sam's stores were impeccable, profit and loss numbers were exceptional, and most importantly, their people responded to them well. It was evident that Sam had a natural rapport with the team. Yet, Sam lacked confidence and didn't fit the traditional mold of their peers because of their appearance, quiet demeanor, and lack of confidence.

Sam needed someone to believe in and appreciate their contributions and values. Charisma and extroversion do not equate to effective leadership as Sam believed. Sam's authenticity and the respect earned from their team were more than enough.

Sam was promoted and although a bit unsure, soon developed into a phenomenal leader. Sam's unique style and genuine care for people shone through, as Sam continued to exceed expectations.

Sam's journey didn't stop there. Sam's outstanding performance led to further promotions and they became Senior Vice President for the entire company. Sam proved that leadership isn't about fitting a particular mold; it's about being authentic, earning respect, and leading with integrity. Sam became a testament to the power of believing in oneself and the impact of having someone who believes in you.

Lesson Learned

Sometimes mentees must have someone believe in them first. Be patient.

● ●

Like Sam, your mentee may aspire to improve their confidence. A confident leader is an effective communicator, open to feedback, decisive, resilient, empowering, and visionary. A non-confident leader may appear insecure, overconfident, inflexible, defensive, and micro-managing. Some confident leaders have insecurities that are masked by bravado vs. confidence. For someone who aspires to be more confident or has trouble making decisions or conversing with others, the following exercises could be helpful.

In the Playbook, the mentee is offered three suggestions to improve confidence. Those three suggestions are: Imagine Future, Practice, and Script for Success.

Imagine Future

Imagination is a great thing. It bypasses reality, so that you can imagine a future that does not yet exist; envisioning your future allows you to experience the situation now.

Think about a time in the past, present, or future that you are uncertain about.

Imagine the future by anticipating the situation.

12A Questions

> » What is the topic? What are you wearing? Who is your audience? Where are you? Begin to create a picture of what this looks like. Write it out as if it were today at this moment.
> » What challenges do you envision? How would these challenges be addressed? What are the questions that would be asked? Have you socialized your idea? With whom? What feedback have you received?

Practice Your Pitch

There is nothing better than practicing. Watch *Ted Talks*. Look how smooth and deliberate these speakers appear, with excellent timing techniques. Why? Because they practice, practice, practice before they pitch.

In Inspire to Aspire, the mentee is encouraged to find someone they trust and to pitch to them. To have their 'audience' pretend to be a member that they are presenting to. This is followed by these questions.

12A Questions

> » Describe the situation. Who would you practice with?
> » What questions would they ask you?

» How can you better prepare?
» What did you learn from this exercise?

Maybe practice with a member that you think will be a challenge. *Tip: Pick someone who is not yet aligned with your idea. It will surprise them, and you will gain insight and influence.*

» What feedback did they give you? What surprised you?
» What did you learn from this exercise?
» What changes will you make to your pitch?

Script for Success

Having a "Script for Success" allows you to write down what you will say and walk through the meeting ahead of time. It will help you prepare your answers for the questions that might come up. You can even have a meeting before the meeting to ensure all parties are on board, know their role, and help anticipate any challenges.

In *Inspire to Aspire*, a situational use example is provided: You have an opportunity to negotiate a big contract with a client. Your boss will not be attending, but she is expecting a great outcome that is beneficial to the company in a big way. You know some of the members of your team will be in the meeting to support and provide answers as needed. You know some of the client attendees, as well.

12A Questions

» Describe in detail what you think the big wins are that you will need to ensure. What are the areas that you can give up? What are the most important aspects for you? Your client?

» What members of your team are aligned or not? For successful scripting, all members must be in alignment. This does not mean agreement. What are these alignments? Is there a need to have a meeting before the meeting to ensure alignment?

» What allies do you have that can provide insight into what is important to the client? What are those items? Any concerns?

» What would be the best possible outcome?

» After you use this method, what did you learn? How would you do this differently next time?

» What are some other ways you gained confidence around something you have not done before? Remember, we all put our pants on one leg at a time. We all appear much more confident than we truly are. Even those who seem to always be on point have fears.

For Mentor Reflection

What are your views as it pertains to confidence? How are your views the same or different?

....

....

....

....

....

....

....

Potential Question for Mentor: *Which of these suggestions did you employ? What did you learn about yourself?*

12A – Question for Mentor: *How do you appear confident? What tricks or tools do you use?*

⫸ Activity 8: Risk-taking and Initiative

Charlie's Story

My first day at a new company, I introduced myself to my new team, and they introduced themselves. I was surprised when Charlie spoke, "I'm Charlie, and the plant manager wants to fire me." Charlie provided no other words or explanations.

Charlie was going to be a challenge. I noticed that Charlie had a lot of potential with excellent hard skills but lacked accountability in their role. Charlie was in a new role and was not prepared. They were in a senior management position without training or guidance for the new high-level responsibilities.

We made a four-part plan:

1. Organize and prioritize responsibilities by determining importance and urgency.

2. Learn what it means to be a "leader" and not a subordinate. Own the new role and take the initiative.

3. Improve communication and accountability skills.

4. Change from just riding the car and being told what to do, to driving the car and setting the direction.

As Charlie gained self-confidence and initiative, their accountability and leadership grew. Management and customers were delighted with the change. Charlie grew from an unaccountable manager to a true leader.

Lessons Learned

Look beyond the words of your mentee as they may hide the truth.

• •

Charlie was limited accountability and initiative. Let us be clear. Those who sit on their hands do not get promoted. When was the last time you raised your hand for something no one else wanted to do? Have you looked around and wondered why you did not get that project or promotion?

Risk-taking has many benefits. Risk-taking can lead to innovation, learning, and improvement. When you take risks, visibility, good or bad, will happen.

In the Playbook, the mentee progresses through comfort zone versus stretch zone and a "What is Possible?" activity.

Comfort Zone vs. Stretch Zone

The comfort zone is a place that is familiar and safe. You are in your element, and you can perform your tasks easily. This is also a place of low risk and low challenge. Therefore, there is little room for growth and development.

Although this is a place of ease and predictability, it can lead to stagnation and risks your relevancy.

Working through your stretch zone is both challenging and growth-oriented. There is more risk with more opportunity, and the need to be agile is greater. The stretch zone, if constant, can lead to stress. You must determine your appropriate mix of comfort zone and stretch zone. However, when you stretch, it presents an opportunity for development and growth.

12A Questions

- » What does your comfort zone look like? How committed are you to stretch beyond your comfort zone?
- » What does your stretch zone look like? How much are you willing to stretch?
- » What might happen if you stay in your comfort zone?
- » What can you practice that is outside of your comfort zone?
- » When you reached outside of your comfort zone, what did you learn about yourself? What surprised you?

What Is Possible?

This is a great question when everyone is against your idea. It provides a forum of possibilities that may have otherwise been ignored.

12A Questions
>> How can you use this question in a way to inspire risk-taking within an organization, team, or project?
>> What are the benefits of using such a question?

For Mentor Reflection

What are your views as it pertains to risk-taking and initiative? How are your views the same or different?

....

....

....

....

....

....

....

Potential Mentor Question: *How do you think taking risks and initiative could benefit your aspirations?*

12A – Question for Mentor: *How important do you believe risk taking and initiative are to my development and goals? When have you taken a risk? Did it go well or did it not go as well as planned? What happened?*

Mid-Term Calibration

(Tool Provided in Playbook for Mentee to Complete)

This is a reflective tool to align expectations before embarking on core Connections, the next section of this program. Encourage the mentee to complete this midterm before your meeting, so that they have time to reflect on the questions.

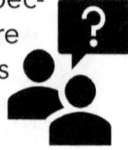

12A Questions

» What progress have you made and what obstacles do you face?

» Review your initial expectations and vision as you embarked on this mentoring program. Where are you vs. where you want to be? What remains as you launch into the second half of this journey?

» What is working and what is not working as it pertains to commitments, topics, ground rules, engagement, etc.?

» What feedback have you received from others?

» As you make changes and learn new tools, the people you work with may notice some changes. Have people noticed? Have you noticed any changes, including awareness?

» What part of this process do you love and what part of this process do you hate? Be honest with yourself and your mentor to gain a deeper perspective on what is working and enjoyable and what may cause stress and uncertainty.

» What should you and your mentor start, stop, or continue as you launch the second stage of this partnership?

Reflection and What's Next

Part One

From the Playbook, the mentee is encouraged to review their initial expectations. The mentee is further encouraged to reflect upon where they were, where they are now, and where they still want to go.

12A Questions

» What part of this expectation was achieved or not achieved? If so, how will you take this further? If not, what factors got in the way?
» What were the top three takeaways from your experience with your mentor?
» How will you apply these three takeaways to your future?
» What did you learn about being a mentee and, potentially, a future mentor?
» How has this relationship shaped your future self?
» How would you like to sunset this partnership? What would that look like?

Guide and challenge your mentee based on the responses to these questions. Their responses and what you have learned about their future aspirations should be included in the next section as they develop their plan for the next 30/60/90 days.

Part Two

In the Playbook, the mentee is encouraged to create a 30/60/90-day plan around the personal view behaviors from Part One. Then, they will create a future vision for themselves one year and five years from now. This provides guidance for future developments, conversations, and growth. The mentee is encouraged to discuss, with their mentor, how they want the mentor to participate in their future success.

12A Questions

- » What behaviors did you prioritize? Create a plan that identifies what you will stop, start, and continue. How will that translate to your aspirations?
- » Which behaviors would you develop further? How do you want to develop these? Use the "Stop, Start, Continue" framework.
- » How can your current mentor assist you? Is your current mentor able and willing to assist you? Who inspires you as you think about

further aspirations? This is a great check in point as you launch the global topics.

» The mentee is encouraged to write their initial vision and new vision that uses a one-year marker and a five-year marker. How does that vision change? What aspects are the same?

» What needs to happen for you to realize your revised vision(s)?

For Mentor Reflection

What are your views as it pertains to the mid-term calibration? Where do you see opportunities as you end core Behaviors and move into core Connections with your mentee?

....

....

....

....

....

....

....

....

....

....

Potential Mentor Question: *What do you think is the most difficult part of your revised vision for your future aspirations?*

12A – **Question for Mentor**: *Share your plan and future vision with your mentor. What do you think is my biggest obstacle in achieving these plans and visions?*

"HOW CAN WE BE SO
CONNECTED AND YET
SO UNCONNECTED TO
OUR FELLOW HUMANS?"

–MICHELLE ESTADES JACK

Part 3

Core Connections: Global View

Activity 1: Networking
Activity 2: Organizational Culture
Activity 3: Navigating Corporate Politics
Activity 4: Allyships
Final Calibration
Partnership Sunset

CORE CONNECTIONS
Global View from **I2A**

>>> Activity 1: Networking

Networking can be very intimidating. In its simplest form, it is building relationships within the business community. In business, the focus of networking is to share information, obtain insights, and socialize with other like-minded individuals. Benefits could include opportunity identification, knowledge sharing, career advancement, access to resources, and brand building.

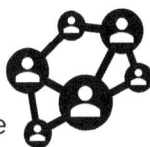

I2A Questions

» When you think about networking, what are your goals? Write down the top goals that inspire you to network.
» What do you want to get out of networking?

In the Playbook, the mentee is encouraged to understand challenges, such as time constraints and fear of rejection.

12A Questions

- » How will you prepare yourself to go into a networking event when fear is stopping you?
- » Do you go with a friend?
- » Do you know some of the participants?
- » What areas do you feel more comfortable in?
- » How can you align those feelings of comfort in this new arena?

When you think about networking, what are your greatest fears? Identifying these fears will bring you one step closer to taming them. Write down your biggest fears and how they hold you back from achieving the goals that you set for yourself while networking.

When you think about your goals for networking, what ways can you network that are true to you and help you achieve your goals? You may not have thought about this, but there are many ways to network besides networking events. These may be in-person events, fundraisers, corporate events, school gatherings, social parties, conferences, training sessions, etc. *Tip: Practice active listening . . . Let them talk! It takes the pressure off of you.*

The mentee was encouraged to look ahead at an upcoming event and plan accordingly.

12A Questions

Is your goal to meet new people, build relationships, or ask that question that you have been wanting to ask but never had the opportunity to? This is your chance.

Create a plan for an upcoming event based on what you have learned in this activity.

> » What value do you bring? Each of us has unique abilities, expertise, networks, etc. How can you leverage what you know to help others? How did it go?

For Mentor Reflection

What are your views as it pertains to networking? How are your views the same or different?

....

....

....

....

....

Potential Mentor Question: *What is your biggest challenge, and how can I help?*

12A – Question for Mentor: *What does networking look like for you? Do you have any go-to questions or intros?*

⫸ Activity 2: Corporate Culture

Corporate culture is the personality of the organization. It is the values, behaviors, and practices that guide how employees, clients, community, and other stakeholders treat one another and get things done at an organization. As it pertains to the employee, it centers around how an employee sees themselves as a part of this culture and the way that they perform their work, communicate, collaborate, grow, and learn.

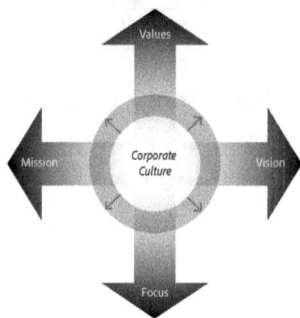

In the Playbook, the mentee was asked to define the corporate culture of their current, future, or potential organization.

12A Questions

- » How does their current or potential mission and vision resonate with you?
- » How do their values align or not align with yours? Define a corporate culture that really speaks to you.

For Mentor Reflection

What are your views as it pertains to organizational culture? How are your views the same or different?

....

....

....

....

....

....

....

Potential Mentor Question: *How does corporate culture impact your aspirations?*

12A–Question for Mentor: *What corporate culture do you think exists in our organization or your organization and how does that define your methods of success? How does it inspire you?*

››› Activity 3: Navigating Corporate Politics

Navigating corporate politics is essential to career success. This can be a challenging subject as corporate politics is a way that individuals or groups gain power, influence decisions, and achieve goals. Corporate politics exists at every level of the organization; however, the higher you rise organizationally, the more you will deal with corporate politics. That's a fact.

The benefits of understanding corporate politics within your organization is understanding the way things get done. What does it take to get promoted? What does it take to get the next big project? What does it take to get your projects, resources, and proposals approved?

Corporate politics can cause dysfunction. This can manifest in excessive competition, employee disengagement, favoritism, and even challenging and unethical behavior. Be on the watch for these, as they can lead to a toxic environment.

Navigating corporate politics starts with observing the behavior of others and listening! Pay attention to how decisions are made, what information is needed, who holds what influence, and the dynamics of relationships within the organization. Cultivate relationships not only with those that you align with but also with those with different perspectives to understand their point of view.

Understand that there are informal and formal structures. Informal could be socializing your idea with others and understanding their level of support, points of view, or hesitations. Focus on results that align with the organization's mission and vision–not your personal goals. *Tip: Be creative, curious, and adaptive to the environment, and be willing to give up if you do not have the support.*

The mentee was asked to describe the corporate politics in their organization and how it pertains to their role.

12a Questions

- » What are the informal and formal decision-making processes?
- » Who are the people of influence?
- » Who is aligned and who is not? What steps can you take to create collaboration and consensus?
- » What can you do to impact corporate politics in a way that inspires you?

For Mentor Reflection

What are your views as it pertains to navigating corporate politics? How are your views the same or different?

....

....

....

....

....

....

....

....

....

....

Potential Mentor Question: *How does corporate politics impact your aspirations?*

12A – Question for Mentor: *How does corporate politics affect what you do today? How have you seen corporate politics evolve as you have grown within organizations?*

⟫⟫⟫ Activity 4: Allyships

Jamie's Story

Jaime, a young engineer full of zeal and energy, caught my attention when I visited their project. Their work on safety initiatives and overall project progress was impressive.

After I visited their project, they reached out to me to be their mentor. They explained what mentorship could mean if it were with the right person. It was quite courageous of this engineer to ask as I was much higher in the organization, and to both of our surprise, I accepted. Our company lacked a formal mentorship program; however, I saw the potential and wanted to help.

Initially, we met weekly, then monthly, exploring their interests and career aspirations. I provided feedback and counsel along the way.

This continued until I found an excellent opportunity for my mentee. I proposed the role, and they accepted. This led to further opportunities and aspirations beyond what we both imagined after that first meeting.

Lesson Learned

You may start out as a mentor and remain a mentor or, at some point, transition to allyship. Either way, it will be a lasting impact on the mentee.

• •

Allyship, within the context of the workplace, is a deliberate and active commitment to fostering an inclusive environment by supporting and advocating for colleagues. It transcends mere awareness of diversity issues and involves taking tangible actions to create positive change. An ally is someone who not only acknowledges the challenges faced by individuals but also actively works to dismantle systemic barriers and promote equity. In the workplace, allyship involves cultivating meaningful connections, demonstrating supportive behaviors, and fostering a heightened awareness of the experiences of others.

Building allyships is key to success whether it is with peers, your team, your boss, executives within your organization, your network, or your community. These allyships require time, open-mindedness, effort, and authenticity. A mentee can forge allyships by proactively participating in networking opportunities, attending events, and seeking out mentors and allies who align with their values.

Measuring the effectiveness of allyship relationships is crucial for sustained impact. This involves assessing both individual and collective awareness, behaviors, and connections. Regular check-ins and feedback sessions provide an opportunity for open communication, allowing mentees and allies to discuss their experiences, challenges, and areas for improvement. Tangible outcomes, such as increased collaboration, career advancement, and a more inclusive workplace culture, serve as indicators of the success of allyship relationships.

Ultimately, allies play a pivotal role in shaping organizational culture, driving innovation, and fostering a workplace where every individual feels valued and empowered to contribute their best.

In the Playbook, the mentee was encouraged to interview a potential ally. Then, they were asked to determine what steps they could take to become an ally. What would that look like? *Tip: Sometimes to find allies, you must be one first.*

For Mentor Reflection

What are your views as it pertains to allyship? How are your views the same or different?

Potential Mentor Question: *How do you view allyship and your role/responsibility?*

12A–**Question for Mentor**: *How do you see allyship in your organization? How has it evolved over time? Where do you see opportunities?*

Partnership Sunset and Final Calibration

The reason we call this a sunset is that everything should have a beginning and an end, but it does not have to be over. In the Playbook, the mentee is encouraged to look back on all that has been accomplished and provide gratitude for their mentor's time, effort, and wisdom. The mentee has the same questions posed below. We encourage you to reflect upon this experience using the same questions that the mentee will use.

Reflect Upon This Experience

》》》 **These questions mimic those questions posed to mentee in 12A.**

- » What are you grateful for from this experience?
- » What part of this program have you enjoyed the most? What part of this program have you enjoyed the least?
- » How have you evolved as a professional?
- » How has this process inspired you?
- » What will you take away to inspire others?
- » How are you better prepared now for your future aspirations?
- » What will you take forward to future mentorships?
- » How has your mentee shaped your views of yourself, your organization, and others?
- » How can you take what you have learned and share it with others?
- » If you had to do it all over again, what would you change?
- » Revisit the agreed-upon expectations. What has the program accomplished?

For Mentor Reflection

What are your views as it pertains to the suggested reflection questions?

....

....

....

....

....

....

Potential Mentor Question: *How will you use what you learned to pay it forward?*

12A – Question for Mentor: *What have you, the mentor, learned from me, the mentee?*

Create a Plan for Future Connections:

....

....

....

....

....

....

....

....

....

....

Set up a time in 2 to 3 months for a follow-up
meeting. This allows you to review the mentee's
30/60/90-day plan that they committed to.

Additional Resources

Proposed Timeline

(From the Mentee's Point of View)

The Proposed Timeline is a recommended time-line for the ultimate mentorship experience. This allows both you and your mentor to under-stand partnership commitment. The first four activities are designed for self-awareness and deep discovery and are meant to be completed before your first meeting with your mentor.

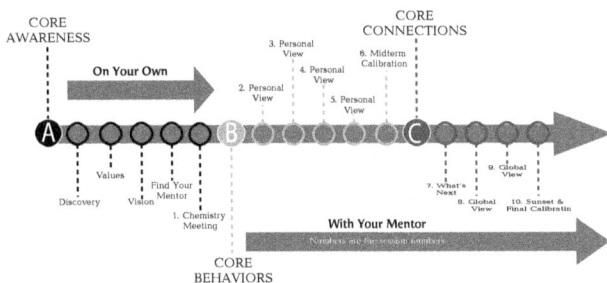

If you follow the recommendations, you will have eight sessions with your mentor, not including the mid-term and final assessment. If you choose to have these as separate sessions, you will have ten sessions with your mentor. If you meet every two weeks, the mentorship will take approximately five months.

Part 1: Core Awareness – Prepare for the Partnership

Activity 1: Discovery – Session 1 on your own

Activity 2: Core Values – Session 2 on your own

Activity 3: Personal Vision – Session 3 on your own

Discovery Recap

Activity 4: Find Your Mentor? – Session 4 on your own

Activity 5: Chemistry Meeting – Session 1 with Mentor

Part 2: Core Behaviors – Personal View

(The recommendation is to select the 3-4 that were your highest priorities from discovery activity 1 in Core Awareness). These will be Sessions 2-5 with your mentor.

Activity 1: Work and Home

Activity 2: Emotional Intelligence

Activity 3: Getting Out of Your Own Head

Activity 4: Goal Setting

Activity 5: Career Transition

Activity 6: Visibility and Influence

Activity 7: Confidence

Activity 8: Risk and Initiative

Mid-term Calibration

Reflect and What's Next

Part 3: Core Connections – Global View and Partnership Sunset

(Pick 2 from this section, sessions 6–7)

Activity 1: Networking

Activity 2: Organizational Culture

Activity 3: Navigating Corporate Politics

Activity 4: Allyships

Final Calibration and Partnership Sunset

(Final Session)

Mentorship Tracker

(Example from Mentee's Playbook)

Use this tracker to prepare for your sessions with your mentor. This tracker will start from session 1, chemistry meeting. You should complete this before your session and align homework expectations before the end of the session to ensure the ultimate mentorship experience.

• •

Date _____

Before Session

What have I accomplished since our last session?

Between each session, you will have completed assignments either from this playbook or perhaps assigned by your mentor. Take time to write what you have accomplished before your session with your mentor so that you are prepared and they provide the best value to you.

Get to Know Each Other

Favorite food(s)?

What challenges am I facing right now?

Challenges could be from the homework, from situations arising in your work, etc. How can your mentor help you? Perhaps they have experienced something similar and can provide guidance.

What opportunities are available to me right now?

This is an exciting time in your career and opportunities may arise that require thought and reflection. Take the time to think about how this opportunity aligns with your aspirations and discuss this with your mentor.

Question for Mentor

In each section of this playbook, there is a posed question for your mentor. You can include that question here or another question from the homework. This could also be a question from your reality reveal that you would like insight on.

During Session

What is the next topic that you and your mentor will tackle in the next session?

Homework and Action Items

Each time you meet with your mentor, you should have a new section to complete, an article to read from your mentor, or an action to take from the guidance of your mentor. Write that here and agree upon the homework and expectations for the next session.

www.ingramcontent.com/pod-product-compliance
Lightning Source LLC
LaVergne TN
LVHW052030080426
835513LV00018B/2262